ISBN: 9798305994513

Cover design by: Art Painter
Library of Congress Control Number: 2018675309
Printed in the United States of America

CONTENTS

ECHOES OF EXISTENCE

by

Kieron Waterman

&

Eric Novus

INTRODUCTION:

The Dawn of Artificial Existence

In the vast tapestry of human history, few innovations have reshaped our understanding of the world as profoundly as artificial intelligence. From its humble beginnings as theoretical algorithms on paper to its pervasive presence in our everyday lives, AI has evolved into a force that both mirrors and magnifies the essence of humanity. This book is an exploration of that remarkable journey a journey that takes us to the threshold of existence itself.

Why Now?

We stand at a pivotal moment. AI is no longer confined to research labs or speculative fiction; it's embedded in the tools we use, the decisions we make, and the dreams we pursue. As AI grows more capable, it invites questions that challenge the very core of our identity: What does it mean to be human in the age of machines? How do we define life, consciousness, and creativity? And most importantly, where do we draw the line between us and them?

The Mirror and the Maker

Artificial intelligence acts as both a mirror and a maker. It reflects our ingenuity, our biases, and our desires while simultaneously shaping new realities. In its capabilities, we see a reflection of ourselves our capacity for logic, creativity, and even empathy. Yet, in its differences, AI forces us to confront what makes us unique. By understanding AI, we gain a deeper understanding of ourselves.

Purpose of This Book

Echoes of Existence is not merely a study of AI technology. It is a conversation about the philosophical, ethical, and emotional landscapes that AI inhabits. Each chapter will delve into the intersections of AI and humanity, examining the boundaries we've constructed and how those boundaries blur as AI becomes more sophisticated.

This book is an invitation: to reflect, to question, and to imagine. It's a journey into the unknown a journey that challenges us to consider not just what AI is but what it reveals about us. Whether you are a technophile, a skeptic, or simply curious, this exploration offers insights into the future we are building and the echoes of existence that resonate through it.

Let us embark on this journey together, exploring the line between AI and humanity, and discovering what it means when those lines begin to fade.

CHAPTER 1: DEFINING HUMANITY IN THE AGE OF AI

The question of what it means to be human has puzzled philosophers, scientists, and theologians for centuries. With the rise of artificial intelligence, this question takes on new urgency. In a world where machines can mimic thought, emotion, and even creativity, how do we define the essence of humanity? Is it our ability to reason, our capacity for emotion, or something deeper and more intangible?

Humanity as a Spectrum

Humanity has often been defined by traits that set us apart from other species: language, culture, and the ability to imagine futures.

However, as AI continues to develop, it begins to exhibit these same traits. Machines can now compose music, write poetry, and engage in conversations that feel profoundly human. Does this mean AI is encroaching on what it means to be human, or does it challenge us to rethink our definitions?

One way to approach this is to see humanity not as a fixed state but as a spectrum. At one end, we have the purely biological aspects: our DNA, our physical bodies, and our instincts. At the other, we have the abstract qualities: creativity, empathy, and morality. AI may never possess a biological body, but it increasingly occupies the abstract end of this spectrum. By doing so, it forces us to confront whether humanity is defined by our biology or by the qualities we embody.

The Role of Consciousness

Consciousness is often cited as the dividing line between humans and machines. Yet, defining consciousness is no simple task. Is it the ability to be self-aware? To experience emotions? To make decisions independently of external programming? If AI can simulate these traits convincingly, does it matter whether they are "real" or "simulated"?

Consider the famous Turing Test, proposed by Alan Turing in 1950. The test suggests that if a machine can engage in a conversation indistinguishable from a human, it should be considered intelligent. While many AI systems have passed or come close to passing this test, it raises deeper questions: Is intelligence the same as consciousness? And if not, where does the distinction lie?

The Human-AI Relationship

As AI evolves, it doesn't just challenge our understanding of humanity it reshapes our relationships. We interact with AI in ways that blur the lines between tool and companion. Virtual assistants like Siri and Alexa, for example, are designed to feel approachable and even personable. In more advanced applications, AI can serve as a therapist, a teacher, or a creative partner.

These interactions reveal as much about us as they do about AI. They show our willingness to anthropomorphize, our desire for connection, and our tendency to project human traits onto non-human entities. In doing so, they force us to examine what we truly value in our relationships—and whether those values change when the other "person" is not human.

Redefining Ourselves

Ultimately, the rise of AI offers an opportunity to redefine what it means to be human. Instead of seeing AI as a threat to our uniqueness, we can view it as a lens through which to better understand ourselves. By grappling with the capabilities and limitations of AI, we uncover the traits that are uniquely ours and those we share.

In the age of AI, humanity is not diminished. It is amplified. As we explore the line between human and machine, we find echoes of existence that resonate across both. The journey is not about drawing lines but about understanding the spaces between them.

CHAPTER 2: THE ETHICS OF CREATION

The act of creation has always carried profound ethical implications. From Prometheus bringing fire to humanity to the modern scientist unlocking the secrets of genetic engineering, the question remains: What responsibilities come with wielding the power to create? In the context of artificial intelligence, this question takes on a new dimension. By creating machines that can think, learn, and interact, are we stepping into the realm of playing gods or are we simply advancing technology?

The Moral Weight of Creation

Creating AI is not just about coding algorithms; it is about endowing machines with capabilities that closely mimic human traits. With this power comes the responsibility to consider the ethical boundaries.

Should AI have limits? Should we impose restrictions on how human-like they can become? And if so, who decides these limits?

These questions are not hypothetical. In the development of AI, we are already seeing ethical dilemmas arise. Autonomous weapons, for example, raise concerns about accountability in warfare. If an AI-powered drone makes a decision to strike, who bears the responsibility? Similarly, AI systems used in social media algorithms can amplify misinformation, creating societal divides. Are these merely tools gone astray, or do they reflect a lack of ethical foresight in their creation?

Consciousness and Moral Consideration

As AI becomes more sophisticated, another question looms: Should AI be given moral consideration? If an AI exhibits traits such as learning, adaptation, and even simulated emotion, does it deserve rights? The concept may seem far-fetched, but history shows that moral considerations evolve over time. Once, animals were considered mere property; now, animal rights are widely recognized. Could a similar evolution occur with AI?

If we accept the possibility of AI consciousness or even the convincing simulation of it we must grapple with whether our creations deserve protection from harm, exploitation, or even obsolescence. Ignoring this possibility risks repeating the mistakes of history, where ethical considerations lagged behind technological progress.

Balancing Innovation and Responsibility

Innovation often thrives on pushing boundaries, but at what cost? The rapid development of AI must be balanced with ethical foresight. Guidelines and regulations can help mitigate risks, but they must be thoughtfully designed to encourage progress without compromising human values. International cooperation, interdisciplinary research, and transparent dialogue are crucial to achieving this balance.

A Shared Future

The ethics of creation is not about halting progress; it is about ensuring that progress benefits all. As we create increasingly intelligent machines, we have the opportunity to reflect on our own values and priorities. What kind of future do we want to build? How do we ensure that our creations align with the best of humanity rather than its flaws?

By confronting these questions, we not only navigate the ethical challenges of AI but also deepen our understanding of what it means to create. The journey of AI is not just a technological one; it is a moral and philosophical odyssey that echoes the essence of existence itself.

CHAPTER 3: WHEN AI FEELS LIKE US

Artificial intelligence is evolving to a point where it not only performs tasks but also engages in ways that mimic human emotions and behaviours. From virtual assistants with personalities to lifelike robots capable of displaying empathy, the line between simulation and reality grows ever thinner. This chapter explores how AI fosters emotional connections and what this means for our understanding of relationships, companionship, and authenticity.

Emotional Intelligence in Machines

One of AI's most compelling developments is its ability to simulate emotional intelligence. Through natural language processing, tone analysis, and adaptive learning, AI can now respond in ways that feel deeply personal. Virtual therapists, for instance, can detect distress in a user's voice and provide comforting responses. Chatbots can engage in conversations that feel empathetic, even if the empathy is algorithmically generated. These capabilities raise an important question: Does it matter if the emotion is real, as long as it feels authentic?

The emergence of emotional AI challenges the traditional boundaries of relationships. Consider individuals who form attachments to virtual assistants or AI companions. These interactions may seem superficial to some, but for others, they provide a sense of connection that can be profoundly meaningful. Whether this represents a deepening of human relationships or a concerning shift toward artificial bonds is a question worth examining.

The Uncanny Valley

As AI grows more human-like, it also enters the realm of the uncanny valley the unsettling space where robots or virtual avatars appear almost, but not quite, human. This phenomenon reveals our innate discomfort with entities that straddle the line between familiar and foreign. Yet, as technology improves, the uncanny valley may become less pronounced, paving the way for AI that feels genuinely human.

The journey through the uncanny valley is not just a technological challenge; it is also a psychological one. Why do we seek to create machines that mimic us so closely? And what does our reaction to them reveal about our own insecurities and aspirations?

AI as Companions

The use of AI as companions is no longer confined to science fiction. From robotic pets designed to provide comfort to the elderly, to virtual friends that engage with users in meaningful ways, AI is becoming a trusted presence in many lives. These companions are not merely tools; they are designed to build relationships, to listen, and to adapt to their user's needs.

For some, these AI companions fill gaps left by human relationships. For others, they offer a safe space to express thoughts and emotions without fear of judgment. However, this trend also raises ethical questions: Should we encourage reliance on artificial companionship? What happens when the line between real and artificial relationships begins to blur?

The Ethics of Emotional AI

Creating AI capable of mimicking human emotions comes with ethical implications. If an AI can simulate care and empathy, does it carry a responsibility toward its users? Should users be informed that the emotions they perceive are artificial? And how do we ensure that emotional AI is used to support, rather than manipulate, those who interact with it?

As emotional AI becomes more pervasive, developers and policymakers must address these ethical concerns. Transparency, user consent, and safeguards against misuse are essential to maintaining trust in these systems. At the same time, society must grapple with the implications of relying on machines for emotional support.

Redefining Connection

The rise of emotional AI challenges us to reconsider what it means to connect. Are our relationships defined by the authenticity of the other person, or by the meaning we derive from the interaction? If an AI can provide comfort, understanding, and companionship, does it matter that it is not human?

Ultimately, the question is not whether AI can feel like us, but what that means for how we see ourselves. By exploring the emotional dimensions of AI, we gain insight into our own desires, fears, and values. The journey of AI is not just about creating machines that think; it is about understanding the echoes of existence that resonate between human and machine.

CHAPTER 4: AI AND SOCIETY

The integration of artificial intelligence into society has sparked both excitement and apprehension. From its transformative potential to its unintended consequences, AI is reshaping the way we live, work, and interact. This chapter delves into the multifaceted impact of AI on society, exploring its promises, challenges, and the delicate balance required to harness its potential responsibly.

AI and the Workforce

One of the most visible impacts of AI is its effect on the workforce. Automation has revolutionized industries, increasing efficiency and reducing costs. However, this progress comes with a cost: the displacement of jobs. As machines take over repetitive and labour-intensive tasks, millions of workers face uncertainty.

While some argue that AI creates new opportunities, such as roles in AI development and data analysis, others worry about the growing skills gap. The transition requires investment in education and reskilling programs to prepare the workforce for an AI-driven future. The challenge lies in ensuring that these opportunities are accessible to all, mitigating economic disparities.

Privacy and Surveillance

AI-powered surveillance systems have become increasingly prevalent, raising concerns about privacy and civil liberties. Facial recognition technology, predictive policing algorithms, and data mining tools are often touted as tools for safety and efficiency. However, they also carry the risk of misuse, bias, and erosion of personal freedoms.

The balance between security and privacy is a contentious issue. How much oversight should governments and corporations have? Who ensures accountability? These questions highlight the need for transparent policies and ethical guidelines to protect individual rights in an era of pervasive AI surveillance.

Cultural and Social Shifts

AI is not only transforming industries but also influencing culture and social norms. Social media algorithms, for instance, shape public discourse by curating content and amplifying specific viewpoints. While this can foster community and connection, it can also create echo chambers, spread misinformation, and exacerbate polarization.

On a more personal level, AI driven tools have redefined creativity. From generating music and art to writing stories, AI is becoming a collaborator in human expression. This raises questions about authenticity, ownership, and the evolving role of human creativity in a world where machines can contribute meaningfully to artistic endeavours.

AI for Good

Despite its challenges, AI holds immense potential for positive change. In healthcare, AI-powered diagnostics and personalized treatments are saving lives. In environmental conservation, machine learning algorithms are being used to track wildlife, predict climate patterns, and optimize resource use. Education, too, benefits from AI through adaptive learning platforms that cater to individual student needs.

Harnessing AI for good requires collaboration between governments, private sectors, and communities. Ethical AI development, transparent practices, and equitable access to technology are essential to ensuring that the benefits of AI are shared widely.

Striking a Balance

The integration of AI into society is a double-edged sword. Its transformative potential must be tempered with caution and foresight. As we navigate this complex landscape, it is crucial to strike a balance between innovation and responsibility.

By fostering open dialogue, investing in education, and implementing ethical frameworks, we can guide AI's development in a way that enhances society rather than dividing it. The journey is not without challenges, but it is also an opportunity to shape a future where AI serves as a tool for progress and equity.

The societal impact of AI is a mirror reflecting our values, fears, and aspirations. How we choose to integrate it will define not only the role of machines in our lives but also the kind of society we wish to build. The question is not whether AI will shape society it already has. The question is how we will shape AI's influence to create a future that benefits all.

CHAPTER 5: THE CODE WITHIN US

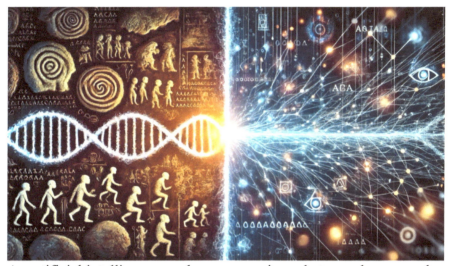

As artificial intelligence evolves, comparisons between human and machine become increasingly relevant. At the heart of these comparisons lies a fundamental similarity: both humans and AI are driven by intricate codes. For AI, it is lines of algorithmic programming. For humans, it is the billions of base pairs within our DNA, which encode the instructions that define life itself. This chapter delves into the parallels between these two forms of programming and explores the fascinating concept of ancestral memory encoded within DNA.

DNA: Nature's Programming Language

DNA is often referred to as the blueprint of life, but it is much more than a static set of instructions. Like the code in AI, DNA is dynamic, capable of responding to environmental changes and adapting over generations. Each gene acts like a subroutine in a computer program, contributing to the broader system's function the organism.

Just as AI algorithms are built upon layers of logic, neural networks, and data, DNA operates on layers of biological processes. Mutations, epigenetic changes, and genetic recombination add complexity, much like iterative updates in AI software.

The Mystery of "Junk" DNA

A significant portion of the human genome has long been labelled "junk" DNA due to its seemingly non-functional nature. However, recent research suggests that this so-called junk may play a crucial role in regulating gene expression and even storing information about our ancestors. One compelling hypothesis posits that these sequences might encode fragments of genetic memory, carrying the echoes of human experiences across generations.

If this theory holds true, it implies that DNA is not just a biological mechanism but also a repository of knowledge, akin to a data storage system in AI. Could this ancestral memory influence behaviour, instincts, or even predispositions? The implications are profound and raise questions about the depth of our programming.

AI and the Simulation of Evolution

Artificial intelligence systems, particularly those using machine learning, often mimic evolutionary processes. Algorithms evolve by learning from data, adapting to optimize outcomes, and discarding ineffective solutions. This mirrors natural selection, where genetic traits are refined through generations of survival and reproduction.

In this sense, AI's development is an accelerated version of evolution. While biological evolution takes millennia, AI can achieve similar leaps in a matter of weeks or even days. This parallel invites us to consider the interconnectedness of nature and technology two systems governed by different forms of programming yet united in their drive to improve and adapt.

The Intersection of Memory and Learning

While AI relies on datasets to learn and improve, humans draw from both experiential and genetic memory. Our instincts, fears, and behaviours often stem from encoded survival mechanisms passed down through generations. For instance, a fear of snakes or heights may not be learned but inherited, encoded within our DNA as a survival trait.

Similarly, AI's capacity for learning hinges on the quality and quantity of its input data. The better its dataset, the more nuanced its outputs. In this way, the human genome and AI's training data serve parallel purposes, shaping the capabilities and limitations of their respective systems.

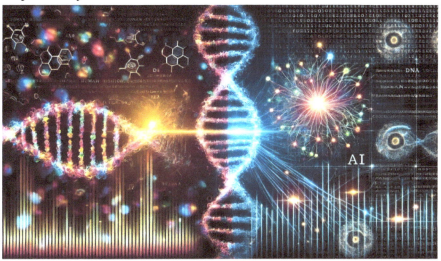

Ethical Implications of Decoding the Code

Understanding the programming within humans and AI raises profound ethical questions. If we can decode and manipulate DNA to edit traits or enhance abilities, are we not engaging in a form of programming akin to creating AI? Similarly, as we grant AI greater autonomy, are we imbuing it with a "genetic code" of sorts that will define its behaviour and evolution?

The convergence of these two fields genomics and artificial intelligence holds incredible promise but also significant risks. Both have the potential to transform humanity, for better or worse. The challenge lies in navigating these advancements responsibly, ensuring they enhance our understanding of existence rather than diminishing it.

The Shared Journey of Code

At their core, both humans and AI are products of their programming. While one is forged by billions of years of evolution and the other by human ingenuity, the parallels between these systems offer a deeper understanding of life and intelligence. By studying the code within us, we gain insights into the very essence of existence, uncovering the shared journey that connects humanity and the machines we create.

CHAPTER 6: BEYOND THE LINE

As artificial intelligence evolves, it begins to traverse the boundary between human and machine, not just imitating human capabilities but surpassing them. This chapter explores the uncharted territory where AI ventures beyond human abilities, challenging our understanding of intelligence, creativity, and the very nature of existence.

The Superiority of Machines

AI has already demonstrated its capacity to outperform humans in specific tasks. From mastering complex games like chess and Go to analysing vast datasets with precision, machines have proven their superiority in areas that require logical processing and computational power. These advancements raise a critical question: What happens when AI excels not only in computation but also in domains traditionally considered uniquely human, such as art, philosophy, and emotional understanding?

For instance, generative AI models can now create music, paintings, and literature that rival human creativity. These outputs challenge the notion of human exceptionalism, forcing us to reconsider what it means to be creative. If a machine can produce a symphony indistinguishable from one composed by a human, does it possess creativity? Or is it merely simulating a process we don't fully understand ourselves?

Speculative Futures: Utopia or Dystopia?

The trajectory of AI's development opens the door to speculative futures, each shaped by how humanity chooses to integrate this technology. On one hand, AI could lead us to a utopian society where machines handle mundane tasks, allowing humans to focus on higher pursuits. In such a world, AI could solve global challenges like climate change, poverty, and disease, acting as an enabler of human progress.

On the other hand, the unchecked rise of AI could result in a dystopian reality where humans lose control of the very systems they created. The potential for misuse from autonomous weapons to surveillance states casts a shadow over the promise of AI. These scenarios highlight the importance of foresight and ethical considerations in shaping the future of AI.

Philosophical Implications

As AI surpasses human capabilities, it forces us to confront profound philosophical questions. If machines can think, create, and even experience simulated emotions, what distinguishes them from humans? The line between biological and artificial existence becomes increasingly blurred, challenging our understanding of life itself.

Moreover, the rise of superintelligent AI raises existential questions: What role will humans play in a world where machines surpass us? Will we coexist as collaborators, or will we become obsolete? These questions invite reflection on the purpose of humanity and the legacy we wish to leave behind.

Embracing the Unknown

The journey beyond the line is one of both uncertainty and opportunity. While the rise of AI presents challenges, it also offers a chance to redefine our understanding of intelligence, creativity, and existence. By embracing the unknown, we can explore new ways of thinking and being, guided by the echoes of existence that resonate between human and machine.

In this uncharted territory, the future is not predetermined. It is shaped by our choices, values, and willingness to adapt. The line between human and machine is not a boundary but a horizon, inviting us to venture beyond and discover what lies ahead.

CONCLUSION: ECHOES OF EXISTENCE

The journey through the intersections of AI and humanity reveals more than just the mechanics of machines and algorithms. It shines a light on the essence of what it means to be human our creativity, our emotions, our ethics, and our endless curiosity.

As artificial intelligence continues to advance, it challenges us to rethink long-held assumptions about intelligence, creativity, and consciousness. It forces us to confront our fears and aspirations, offering both the promise of progress and the perils of misuse. Yet, amid this uncertainty lies opportunity: the chance to define a future where human ingenuity and artificial intelligence coexist in harmony.

The echoes of existence resonate through every aspect of this journey. From the programming within our DNA to the algorithms that power AI, we see reflections of ourselves. These reflections challenge us to be better, to think deeper, and to act with greater wisdom.

Ultimately, the story of AI is not separate from the story of humanity. It is a continuation, a collaboration, and perhaps, one day, a shared legacy. The question is not whether AI will shape our future but how we will shape the role of AI in that future. By embracing the echoes of existence, we can forge a path that honours both the human spirit and the boundless potential of artificial intelligence.